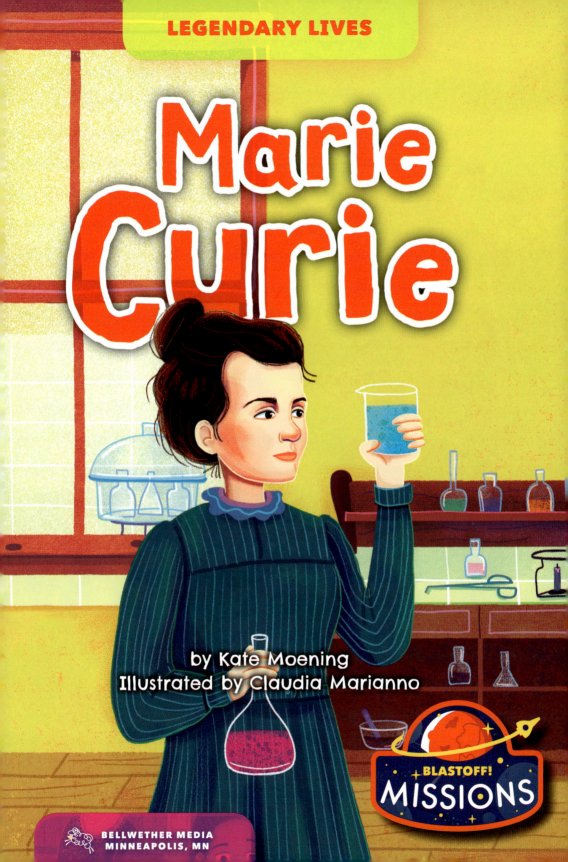

Blastoff! Missions takes you on a learning adventure! Colorful illustrations and exciting narratives highlight cool facts about our world and beyond. Read the mission goals and follow the narrative to gain knowledge, build reading skills, and have fun!

Traditional Nonfiction

Narrative Nonfiction

Blastoff! Universe

MISSION GOALS

> FIND YOUR SIGHT WORDS IN THE BOOK.

> LEARN ABOUT MARIE CURIE'S LIFE.

> LEARN HOW MARIE CURIE'S WORK HELPED SCIENCE.

This edition first published in 2026 by Bellwether Media, Inc.

No part of this publication may be reproduced in whole or in part without written permission of the publisher. For information regarding permission, write to Bellwether Media, Inc., Attention: Permissions Department, 3500 American Blvd West, Suite 150, Bloomington, MN 55431.

Library of Congress Cataloging-in-Publication Data

LC record for Marie Curie available at: https://lccn.loc.gov/2025018595

Text copyright © 2026 by Bellwether Media, Inc. BLASTOFF! MISSIONS and associated logos are trademarks and/or registered trademarks of Bellwether Media, Inc. Bellwether Media is a division of FlutterBee Education Group.

Editor: Rebecca Sabelko   Designer: Andrea Schneider

Printed in the United States of America, North Mankato, MN.

This is **Blastoff Jimmy!** He is here to help you on your mission and share fun facts along the way!

Table of Contents

Meet Marie Curie	4
A Young Scientist	6
New Elements	12
The Work Continues	18
Glossary	22
To Learn More	23
Beyond the Mission	24
Index	24

A Young Scientist

It is the 1870s. Young Marie lives in Warsaw, Poland.

Marie's father teaches her math and science. Marie remembers things easily. She learns quickly!

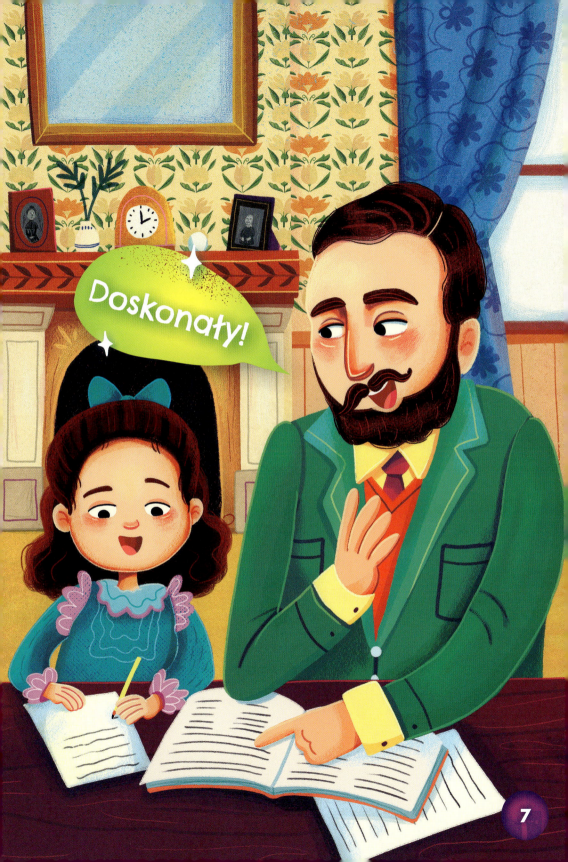

Marie is a scientist. She works in Pierre Curie's lab. He is also a scientist.

Marie and Pierre get married! They become talented work **partners**.

▶ JIMMY SAYS ◀

In 1944, a new element was named for Marie and Pierre! It is called curium.

New Elements

Marie studies **radioactive material**. She and Pierre discover two new **elements**. One is called radium.

Marie and Pierre win a **Nobel Prize** for their discoveries!

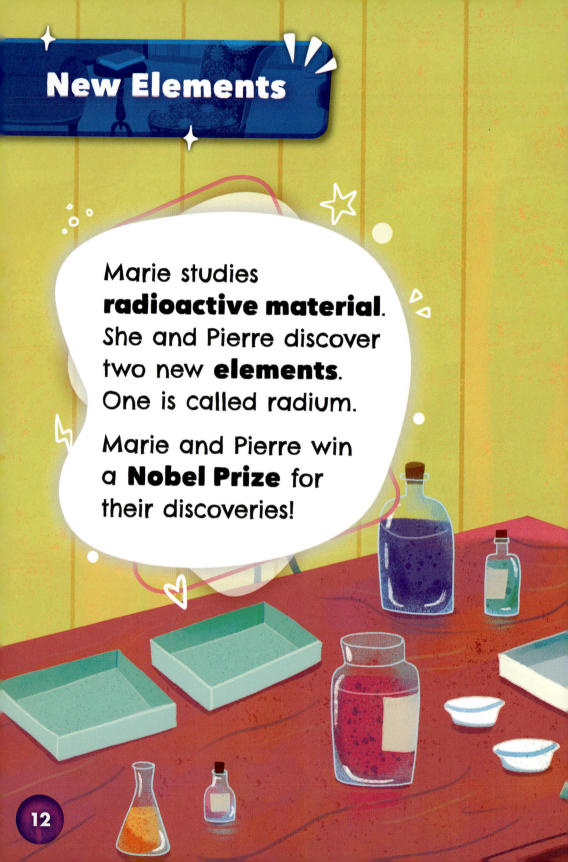

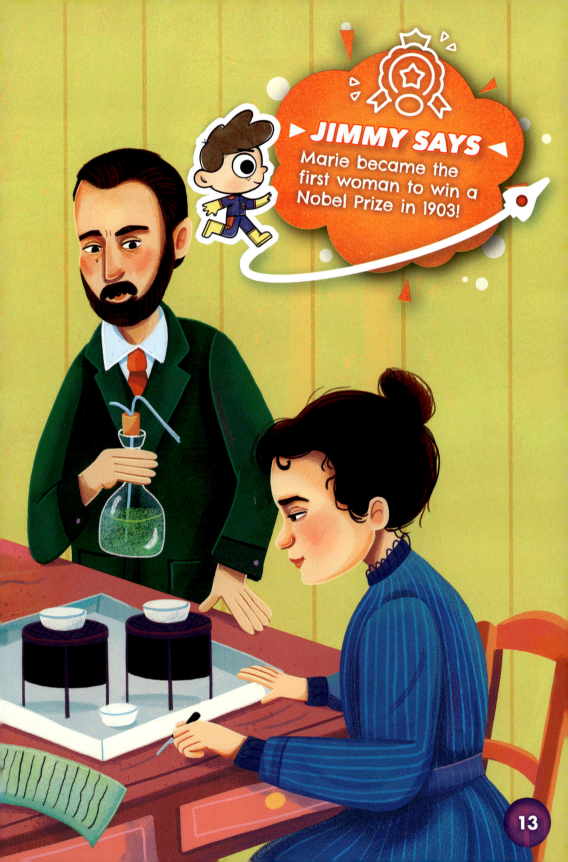

She takes his place teaching at the University of Paris. She is the first woman to teach there!

It is now 1914. **World War I** has begun. Marie wants to help. She builds cars that carry **X-ray** machines.

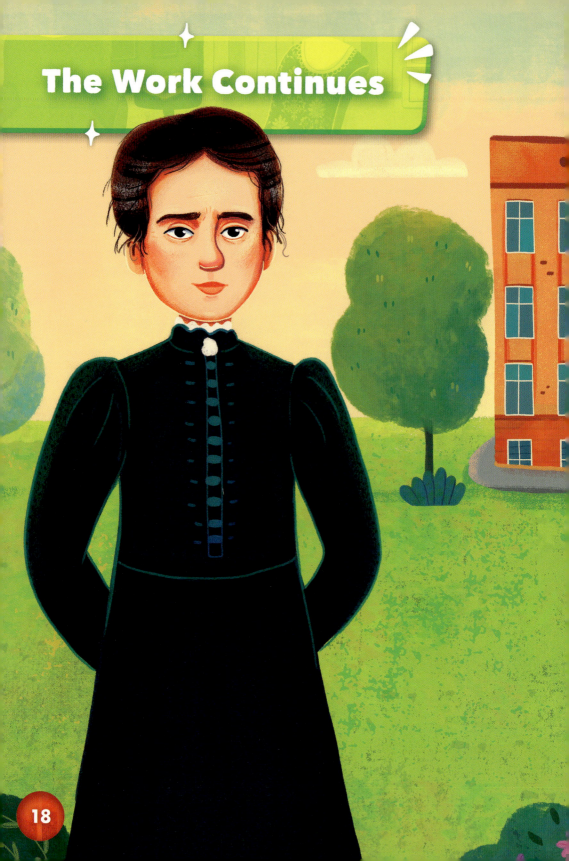

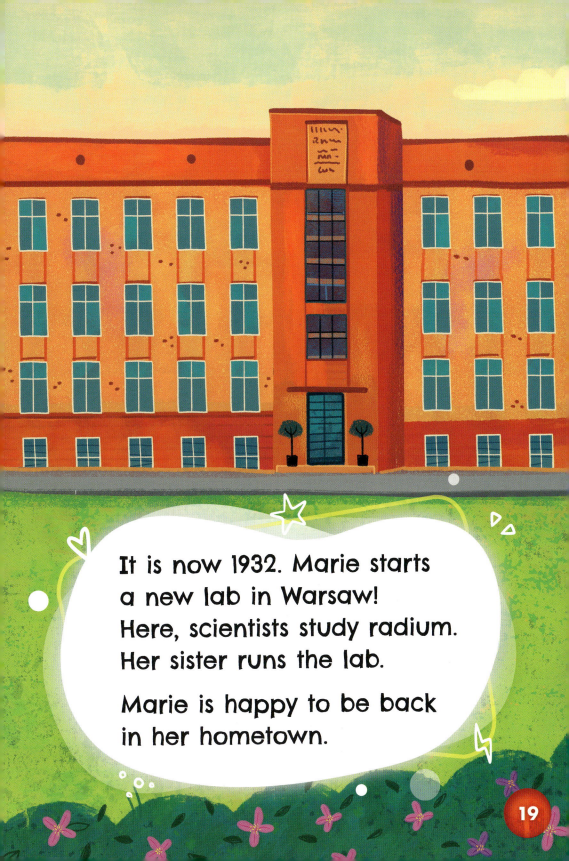

It is now 1932. Marie starts a new lab in Warsaw! Here, scientists study radium. Her sister runs the lab.

Marie is happy to be back in her hometown.

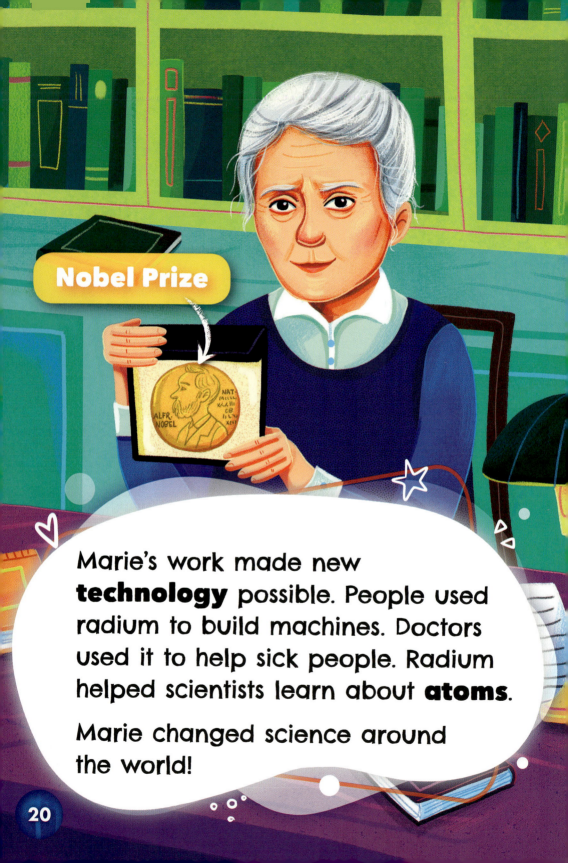

Nobel Prize

Marie's work made new **technology** possible. People used radium to build machines. Doctors used it to help sick people. Radium helped scientists learn about **atoms**.

Marie changed science around the world!

Marie Curie Profile

Born
November 7, 1867, in Warsaw, Poland

Died
July 4, 1934

Accomplishments
Scientist who discovered two new elements and studied radioactivity

Timeline

1894: Marie works in Pierre Curie's lab and the two get married one year later

1898: Marie and Pierre discover two new elements, radium and polonium

1903: Marie and Pierre win the Nobel Prize in Physics with Henri Becquerel

1911: Marie wins the Nobel Prize in Chemistry

1932: Marie opens a radium lab in Warsaw, Poland

Glossary

atoms–the smallest parts of matter

elements–basic matter; elements are made up of only one kind of atom.

Nobel Prize–an important prize awarded each year; Nobel Prizes are given in six different subjects.

partners–people who work together

physics–a science that deals with matter, energy, heat, light, electricity, motion, and sound

radioactive material–matter that produces a powerful type of energy

radium–an element that is radioactive

technology–a tool that solves problems

university–a school that people go to after high school

World War I–the war fought from 1914 to 1918 that involved many countries

X-ray–a photograph made with a special machine to show the inside of the body

To Learn More

AT THE LIBRARY

Hopkinson, Deborah. *Determined Dreamer: The Story of Marie Curie*. New York, N.Y.: HarperCollins Publishers, 2024.

MacCarald, Clara. *Marie Curie: Radiation Pioneer*. Minneapolis, Minn.: Jump!, 2024.

Roesser, Marie. *Elements*. New York, N.Y.: Enslow Publishing, 2026.

ON THE WEB

FACTSURFER

Factsurfer.com gives you a safe, fun way to find more information.

1. Go to www.factsurfer.com.

2. Enter "Marie Curie" into the search box and click 🔍.

3. Select your book cover to see a list of related content.

BEYOND THE MISSION

> WHAT FACT FROM THE BOOK DO YOU THINK WAS THE MOST INTERESTING?

> WHAT WOULD YOU LIKE TO DISCOVER IF YOU WERE A SCIENTIST?

> IF YOU COULD MEET MARIE CURIE, WHAT QUESTIONS WOULD YOU ASK HER?

Index

atoms, 20
Curie, Pierre, 10, 11, 12, 14
curium, 10
doctors, 17, 20
father, 6
lab, 5, 10, 19
math, 6, 8
Nobel Prize, 12, 13, 20
Paris, France, 8, 9, 15
physics, 8
profile, 21

radioactive material, 12
radium, 5, 12, 19, 20
science, 5, 6, 20
scientist, 10, 19, 20
sister, 9, 19
teaches, 6, 15
technology, 20
university, 8, 9, 15
Warsaw, Poland, 6, 9, 19
World War I, 16
X-ray machines, 16, 17